M N
P Q R
S T U
V W X

DIN 1451 MITTELSCHRIFT © 1936 BERTHOLD LINOTYPE LIBRARY

DIN 1451: FONT > BOOK, A PROCESS

GRAPHIC LANGUAGE
PUBLISHED BY PROTOTYPE EDITIONS
WITH KRABBESHOLM HØJSKOLE [DK]
EDITION: 1000 COPIES
ISBN NR: 90-806012-4-1
DISTRIBUTION:
IDEA BOOKS AMSTERDAM

KRABBESHOLM HØJSKOLE
DIN 1451: FONT > BOOK, A PROCESS

1>TYPEFACE
2>WORKSHOP
3>PRACTICE
4>BOOK

GRAPHIC
LANGUAGE
PROTOTYPE
EDITIONS

6

KRABBESHOLM HØJSKOLE
DIN 1451:
FONT > BOOK, A PROCESS

PREFACE BY KURT FINSTEN

INTRODUCTION BY PAUL OUWERKERK

7

GRAPHIC LANGUAGE PROTOTYPE EDITIONS

ISBN 90-806012-4-1

KRABBESHOLM HØJSKOLE

DIN 1451: FONT > BOOK, A PROCESS

GRAPHIC
LANGUAGE
PROTOTYPE
EDITIONS

11-12-00 ___ Dear Paul Ouwerkerk, ___ Poul Mousten Sørensen has told me a lot about your work and shown me some of your books. It looks extremely exciting! The books are very beautiful and to me they seem to forward and update a Bauhaus and De Stijl tradition that is similar to the field in which we are working at Krabbesholm. ___ Krabbesholm is a Danish college of art, architecture and design. We co-operate with artists, architects and designers from both Denmark and abroad. They visit the college and stay here for either short or long periods of time. They involve our students in their work, teach them and give lectures. For further information, please see our website www.krabbesholm.dk. ___ I would like to invite you to come to Krabbesholm to give a lecture on your work. ___ Do you think it might be possible in the beginning of the Spring term? We will pay a fee and refund your travel expensives of course. Maybe you could do some teaching as well (talk to the students and discuss their work with them)? One or two days perhaps. ___ I would really love to welcome you to Krabbesholm and discuss possible future cooperation projects with you. ___ Best regards, ___ Kurt Finsten

KRABBESHOLM
HØJSKOLE
DIN 1451:
FONT > BOOK,
A PROCESS

1>TYPEFACE

10

2>WORKSHOP
3>PRACTICE
4>BOOK

GRAPHIC
LANGUAGE
PROTOTYPE
EDITIONS

How does one deal with a fascination for probably the most nondescript typeface ever to be designed? ___ By investigating its nature. By researching its origin. Through massive application. By making it the point of departure for a workshop. Ultimately, by constructing a book about it. ___ This book tells the story of that fascination with a typeface, and at the same time describes a method of the design and construction of books themselves. ___ It is the translation of a process of design as well as the deconstruction of a myth. To make a book as a composition of elements is to solve a puzzle consisting of contextual and visual pieces. To compose is to comprehend. To compile is to reflect. To visualize is to communicate. ___ Bookmaking as therapy. Design as meditation. ___ Paul Ouwerkerk

KRABBESHOLM HØJSKOLE
DIN 1451:
FONT > BOOK, A PROCESS

GRAPHIC
LANGUAGE
PROTOTYPE
EDITIONS

DIN 1541 Neuzeit Grotesk. ___ In 1917 as part of the [1st World] war effort, the Society of German Engineers formed the German Standards Commitee. In 1922 came the introduction of paper standards, DIN 476 - 'A' series of paper sizes, based on a sheet 1m2 in area, with the length of the sides in ratio to the Golden Rectangle, and hence measured 841 x 1189 mm. Smaller sizes were then produced by sequentially folding the original size.

___ By 1936 the German Standard Committee settled upon DIN 1451 as the standard font for the areas of technology, traffic, administration and business. In 1926 the institute had changed its name to Deutsches Institute für Normung, thus the abbreviation DIN. ___ The DIN 1451 typeface [DIN Mittelschrift and DIN Engschrift] was designed by H. Berthold and copyrights are held by Linotype-Hell AG, a subsidiary of Heidelberger Drückmaschinen AG.

In recent history, Graphic Language has produced variations on a theme; versions of DIN based on the original 1936 typeface. Since the original DIN only featured Mittelschrift and Engschrift, the next step included the development of DIN Bold, Thin and Oblique. DIN Stencil was born out of practical necessity with later versions stemming instead from curiosity itself. These later versions describe more about visual effect than their ties to a particular typeface of origin. Nevertheless, they can be more clearly judged precisely because of that neutrality of origin. ___ The conclusion: Berthold isn't easily beaten.

A B C
D E F

DIN FETTSCHRIFT ©1998 GRAPHIC LANGUAGE

G H I
J K L

M N O
P Q R
S T U
V W X

15

A B C

D E F

DIN DÜNNSCHRIFT ©1998 GRAPHIC LANGUAGE

G H I

J K L

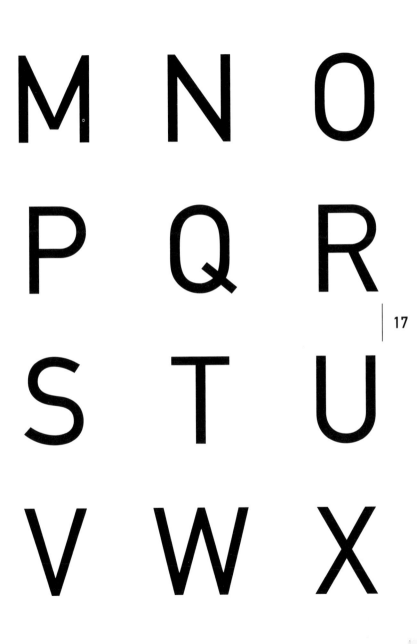

A B C

D E F

DIN MEDIANSCHRIFT ©2000 GRAPHIC LANGUAGE

G H I

J K L

M N O
P Q R
19
S T U
V W X

DIN OFFSETSCHRIFT ©2000 GRAPHIC LANGUAGE

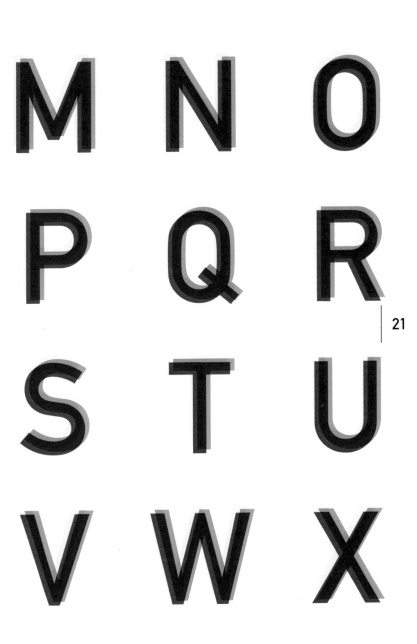

21

DIN VAGESCHRIFT ©1999 GRAPHIC LANGUAGE

A B C

D E F

DIN RUNDSCHRIFT ©2001 GRAPHIC LANGUAGE

G H I

J K L

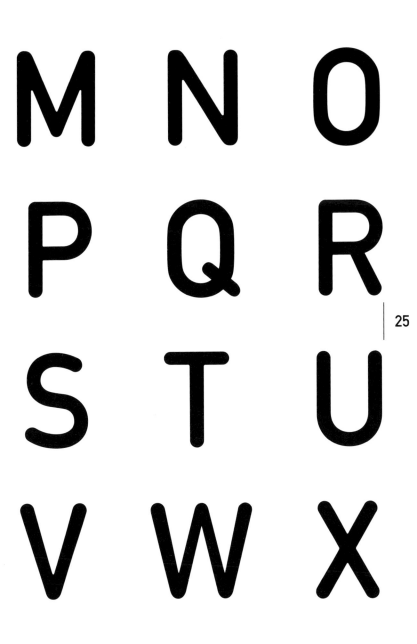

25

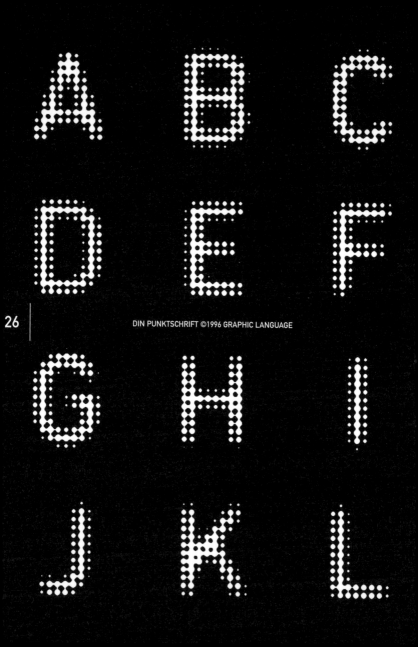

DIN PUNKTSCHRIFT ©1996 GRAPHIC LANGUAGE

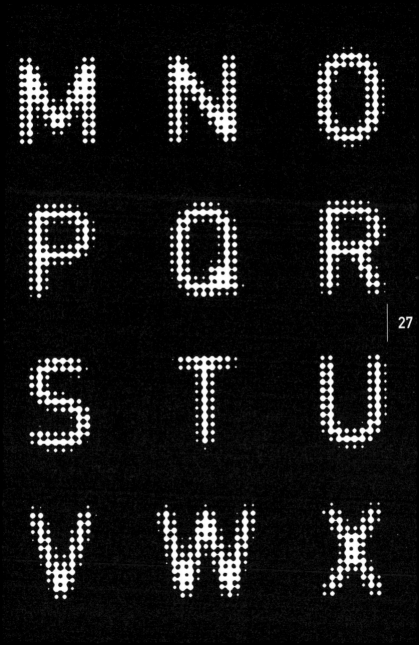

KRABBESHOLM HØJSKOLE DIN 1451:
FONT > BOOK,
A PROCESS
1>TYPEFACE
2>WORKSHOP
3>PRACTICE
4>BOOK
GRAPHIC LANGUAGE PROTOTYPE EDITIONS

The workshop was conducted in a period of 4 days. The attendants were a group of some 20 students of the Krabbesholm Højskole, all of who were 'freshmen' in terms of their exposure to graphic design education. The aim was to create a working environment not unlike the reality of a graphic design practice where time is sliced into segments each defining a different 'mission' and all containing ingredients of the process of design. Writing, researching, inspecting, reviewing, expressing and editing: a crash course in perception and conceptual thinking, through the process of autonomous creation. In the end, all the pieces fall together and form the parts for the construction of a document - a document about the workshop itself. Each student created his/her individual book and these books were then [1, page 38] bound together in a single volume complete with writings, transcripts and documentary images of the workshop creating a 'workbook' available to be consulted by future generations of Krabbesholm students. [2, page 39] Each individual student book was exhibited for critique by everyone involved along with other students and staff.

29

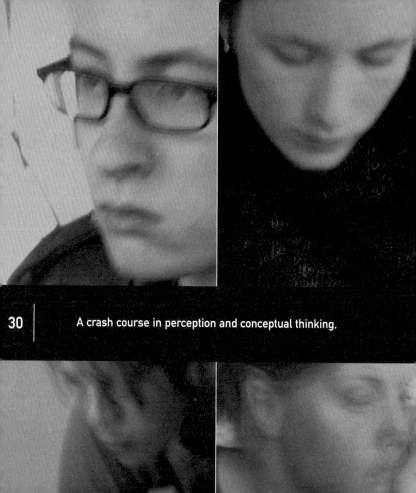

A crash course in perception and conceptual thinking.

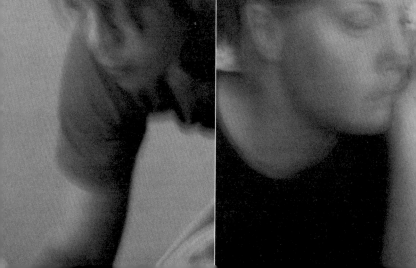

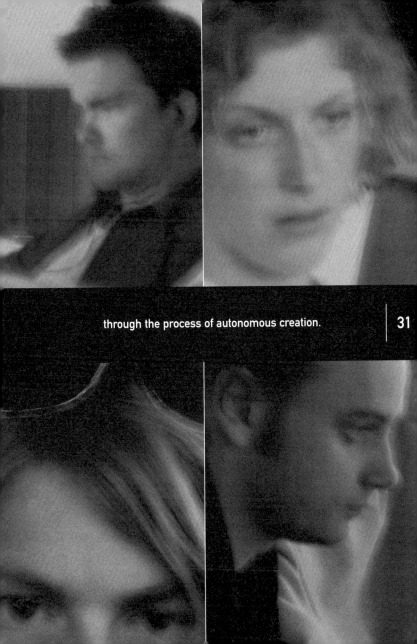

through the process of autonomous creation.

PART 1:

Digital photography
of applied graphics.
4 groups of 5 students each.
4 locations. 4 scales.

1: supermarket
2: gas station
3: bank
4: hospital

A: outside - large scale
B: outside - small scale
C: inside - large scale
D: inside - small scale

PART 3/4:

Application of typeface DIN
Mittelschrift on photographed
location.

Typographic design
Collage [in Photoshop]
Minimum of 4 scales/-
applications

PART 2:

Study of typeface
DIN Mittelschrift
[individual or group].
> Size relationships
> Capital/lowercase
> Positive/negative
> Colour

Part 1 and 2 can be switched
for practical reasons, e.g.
amount of digital cameras.

PART 5:

Write a short essay about the
virtues [or the non-virtues] of
typeface DIN Mittelschrift.
150 words. 25 phrases.
totaling an A5 sheet of text.

PART 7:

Final design of booklet.

PART 6:

Construction of a 24 page A5
[oblong] document in
QuarkXpress.
> Basic layout
> Content in chapters
  Containing:
0: Cover [front/back]
1: Essay
2: Digital photography research
3: Study of typeface
   DIN Mittelschrift
4: Applicatons/Collages
5: Conclusion
6: Credits

PART 8:

1: Assemble books
   into 1 volume.
2: Presentation of all booklets
   on a large wall.

34 | Student work: Study of typeface DIN Mittelschrift.

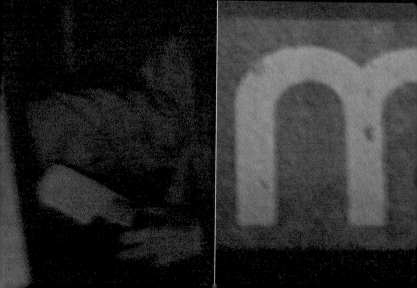

DIN Mittelschrift

DIN. This quasi-legendary abbrevi...
...industrial in the modern, westerniz...
...ese three solitary letters invariabl...
...bility, supporting and furthering th...
...ion and, above all, meticulous atte...
...he universal aplicability of the...
...surprise to see this formal applicat...
...an entire typeface. This typeface. W...
...with fascism, has won a large foll...
...and DIN-approval has given it st...
...Germany. On closer inspection it...
...ravelled the german Autobahn, w...
...tributers to the legend of germani...

KLU

TYPEFACE INVESTIGATION:
SAY OM DIN MITTELSCHRIFT
af Emil M. Brandt

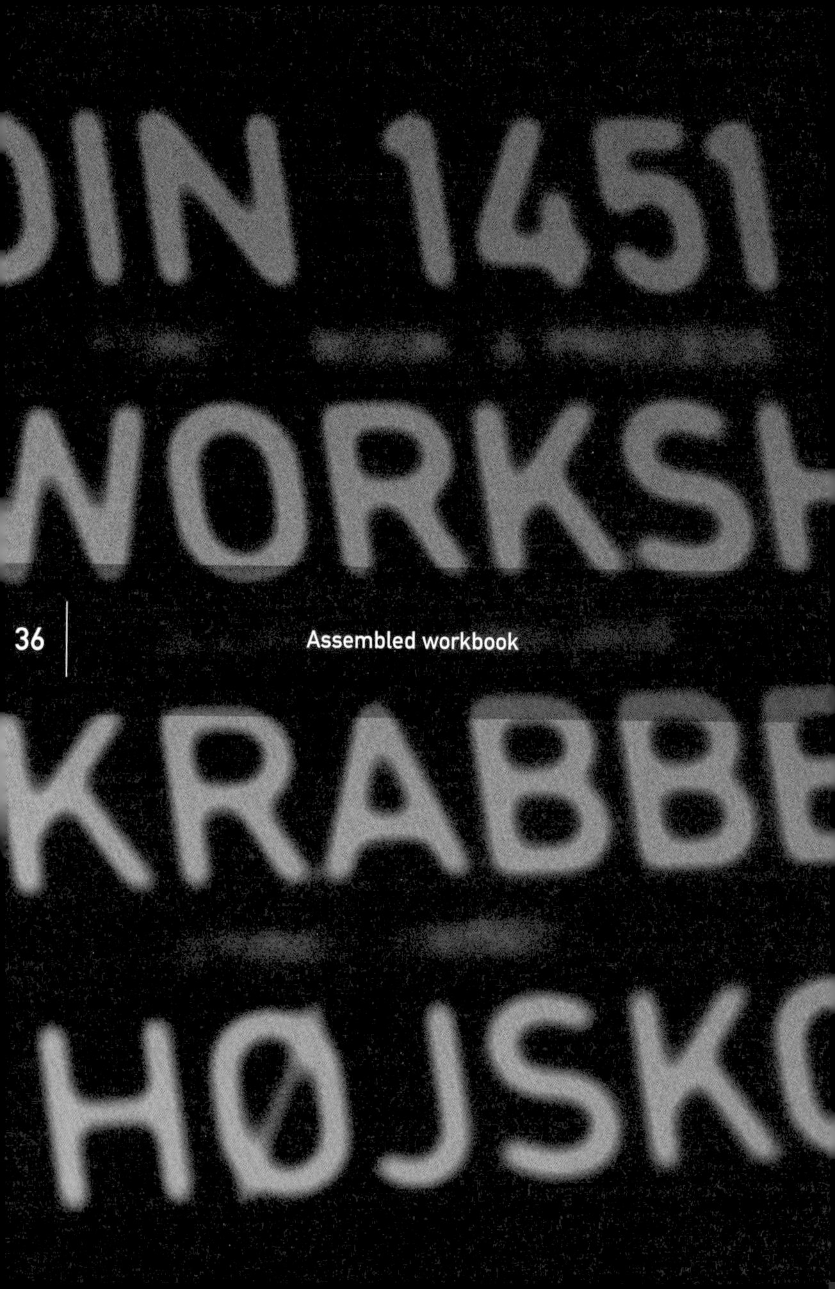

DIN 1451

WORKSH

KRABBE

HØJSKO

Exhibition [Krabbesholm 10052001] | 37

KRABBESHOLM HØJSKOLE DIN 1451:

FONT > BOOK, A PROCESS

1>TYPEFACE

2>WORKSHOP

3>PRACTICE

4>BOOK

GRAPHIC
LANGUAGE
PROTOTYPE
EDITIONS

The following examples show DINspired graphic designs by Graphic Language. ___ p40/p41: The corporate identity for Graphic Language/Prototype Editions consists of a typographical approach in DIN. The company names are written out in lower case with starting capitals. The descenders in both names are cut off by the underlinement. Below that follow the company subtitles. ___ p42/p43: Letters of the greek alphabet were constructed in DIN for the signage system that was conceptualized for OMA's Educatorium building at the University of Utrecht, NL. ___ p44/p45: A deconstructed DIN serves as a kinetic log® in the introduction page of the website for S333 Architecture and Urbanism [s333.org]. This kinetic logo® was animated in Flash®. All typography in the website in DIN Mittelschrift. ___ p46/p47: A book cover for S333 is constructed with the title [3 villas] and the author [S333]. The corporate identity for S333 features the kinetic logo® as a machine that creates its own grid system by sequencing the animation. Typography entirely in 8 pt DIN Mittelschrift. ___ p48/p49: Two book cover designs for Prototype Editions. Din Mittelschrift capitals provide opportunity to either 'unite' or 'exclude'. ___ p50/p51: One of the proposed logos for ING's 'Arena' project in Prague is constructed in horizontal lines, following the shape of the name 'Arena' and written in DIN capitals. ___ p52/p53: Two cover proposals for MVRDV. One for the critically acclaimed publication 'MetaCity DataTown'. And one for a study by Graphic Language, featuring a deconstructed 'logo' of MVRDV as a background.

between complexity and si

ceiver.

phic Langu

ign and consultancy

RLANDS · T: +31 10 433 4340 · F: +31 10 433 2586 · MAIL@PROTOTYPE-EDIT

totype Editi

contemporary p

method, an independent means

eflect but creates at the same

Graphic Language

graphic design & consultancy

Paul Ouwerkerk   designer

Baan 177   T +31 [0] 10 433 4340
3011 CA Rotterdam   F +31 [0] 10 433 2586
The Netherlands

mail@prototype-editions.com
www.prototype-editions.com

Prototype Editions

contemporary publishing

Paul Ouwerkerk   publisher

Baan 177   T +31 [0] 10 433 4340
3011 CA Rotterdam   F +31 [0] 10 433 2586
The Netherlands

mail@prototype-editions.com
www.prototype-editions.com

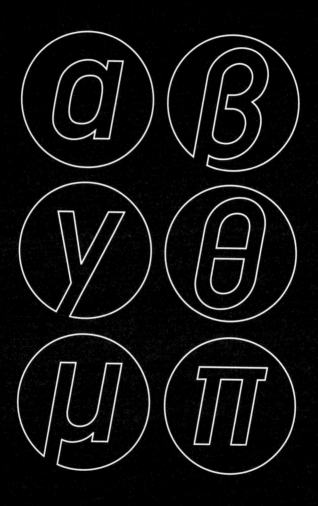

OFFICE FOR METROPOLITAN ARCHITECTURE: SIGNAGE EDUCATORIUM [GL 1997]

96

43

WITTE DE WITHSTRAAT

BAR P: ADDRESS [GL 2002]

S333

STUDIO FOR ARCHITECTURE AND URBANISM

There is a
further benefit of
cross-fertilization
of ideas.

S333

S333

S333

ᴲᴱᴽᴱ

OFFICE STATEMENT

STUDIO

PEOPLE

CONTACT

HISTORY

FACTS

PROJECTS

REFERENCES

45

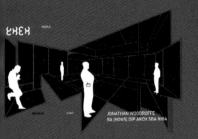

ᴽᴴᴲᴽ PEOPLE

MEMBERS   STAFF   JONATHAN WOODROFFE
BA [HONS] DIP ARCH SBA RIBA

ᙆᙆᙆᙆ   PEOPLE

JONATHAN WOODROFFE
BA [HONS] DIP ARCH SBA RIBA

JONATHAN WOODROFFE IS A FOUNDING PARTNER OF
THE AMSTERDAM PRAKTISE ESTABLISHED IN 1997.

Jonathan Woodroffe [London 1964] studied Architecture at
Portsmouth Polytechnic and at the University of Cincinnati
before graduating in 1990.

In the eight years prior to 1997, Jonathan gained considerable
experience in several top architectural practices including
Wilkinson Eyre in London and Neutelings Riedijk in Rotterdam. During that period he worked on numerous housing
and urbanism projects, and on a wide range of important
landmark buildings including the Stratford Market Depot
London, the Holland House in Gent, the Minnaert Building,
Utrecht and the ASN-AMRO Bank Headquarters in
Amsterdam.

MEMBERS   STAFF

ᙆᙆᙆᙆ   HISTORY

January
February
March
May
June

September
October
November
December

9030   HISTORY

• January
• February
• March
• April
• May
• June
• July
• August
• September
• October
• November
• December

94

Studio 333
participates in
A(topos) debate at
the Architectural
Association in
London

Burton Hamfelt,
Partner

S333
Architecture + Urbanism

Overtoom 197
1054 HT Amsterdam, NL

Tel: +31 (0) 20 412 4194
Fax: +31 (0) 20 412 4187

burtonhamfelt@s333.org
www.s333.org

ƎƧꞦƎ

47

ƎƎƧ2 SS33 ꞦꞨ2Ꞧ ƎƎꞨꞨ SꞦSƎ
ƎꞦSƎ SƎƎƎ ꞦƎƎ2 SƎꞨꞦ SƎYY
SƎƎƎ SꞦꞨꞦ ƎꞨƎꞨ ꞦꞦꞾY ꞦꞦꞦƎ
YꞦꞦY ꞦS33 YꞦSꞦꞨ ƎƎƎƎ SꞦꞨꞦ
ꞨꞨƎƎ Ǝ ꞨꞦꞨ ꞨSSꞦ YꞦꞨꞦ ꞦS33
ꞨSS2 ꞦYꞦꞨ YꞨꞦꞦ 2SƎꞨ ƎƎꞨƎ

48

LOTUS
... STATE OF MIND

PAUL OUWERKERK
PROTOTYPE EDITIONS

SKYSCAPES

PROTOTYPE EDITIONS

VICTOR BURGOS

ARENA

2

'Arena' is an urban regeneration project in the borough of Holesovice, Prague 6 in the Czech republic. The basis is a compound that formerly served as a beer brewery. The objective is to create an environment in which companies can find a dynamic home, a multi-disciplinary program that can catalyze the redevelopment of an entire neighborhood primarily within the compound, and secondarily throughout the district. We see the 'Arena' project as a stone that is dropped in the pond. Its ripples will move far beyond the boundaries of the compound. We are talking about a highly dynamic intervention.

Foodmarkets

GRAPHIC LANGUAGE
PROTOTYPE EDITIONS

META
CITY
DATA
TOWN
MVRDV

010 PUBLISHERS

KRABBESHOLM HØJSKOLE
DIN 1451:
FONT > BOOK, A PROCESS
1>TYPEFACE
2>WORKSHOP
3>PRACTICE
4>BOOK

GRAPHIC
LANGUAGE
PROTOTYPE
EDITIONS

D: DIN 1451   1>: TYPEFACE
M: MENU   2>: WORKSHOP
T: TEXT   3>: PRACTICE
C: CREDITS   4>: BOOK

The storyboard of the content of this book is feaured on page 56 - page 59. The book is structured along a 'spine' that runs from front cover to back cover. This 'spine' is the menu [M] that serves as the book title as well as the subtitle, the content, the chapter headings, the author and the publisher. The text sequence [T] follows naturally. It provides introductions to the project, the book and the chapters. The 4 main chapters [1>, 2>, 3>, 4>] are featured in a linear sequence. The credits [C] are divided and positioned at the start and the end of the book's interior. The book's interior is placed between DIN 1451 Mittelschrift and Engschrift [D], the 1936 versions by Berthold/Linotype Library.

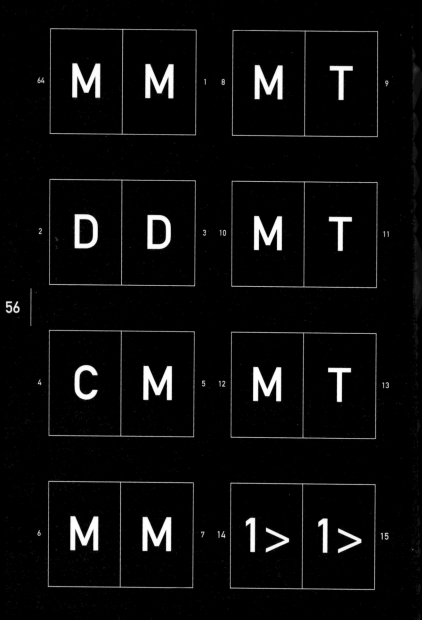

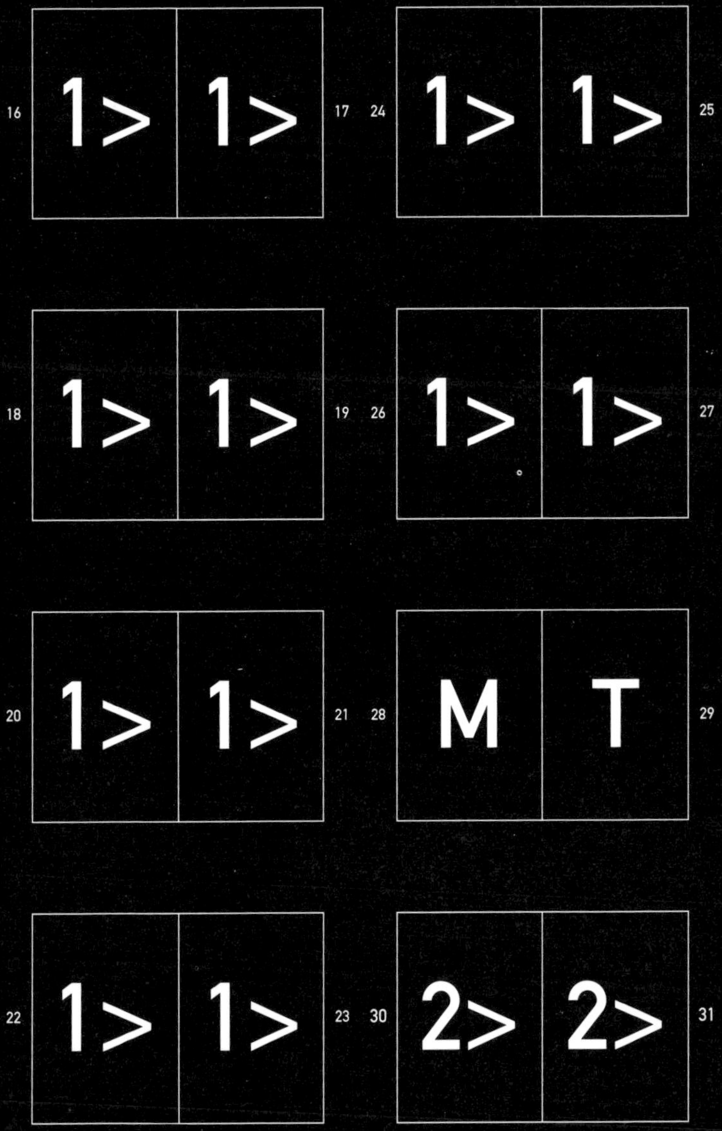
16
1>
1>
17
24
1>
1>
25
18
1>
1>
19
26
1>
1>
27
20
1>
1>
21
28
M
T
29
22
1>
1>
23
30
2>
2>
31

58

32	2>	2>	33	40	3>	3>	41
34	2>	2>	35	42	3>	3>	43
36	2>	2>	37	44	3>	3>	45
38	M	T	39	46	3>	3>	47

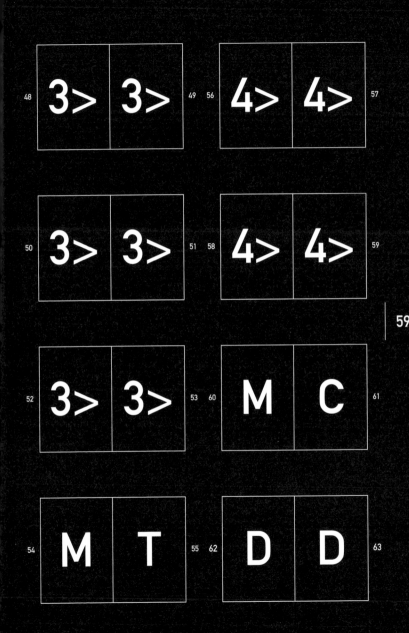

KRABBESHOLM HØJSKOLE DIN 1451: FONT > BOOK, A PROCESS

1>TYPEFACE
2>WORKSHOP
3>PRACTICE
4>BOOK

GRAPHIC
LANGUAGE
PROTOTYPE
EDITIONS

DIN 1451: FONT > BOOK, A PROCESS
PREFACE BY KURT FINSTEN, KRABBESHOLM HØJSKOLE
INTRODUCTION + WORKSHOP BY PAUL OUWERKERK
DIN 1451 MITTELSCHRIFT + ENGSCHRIFT BY H. BERTHOLD
COURTESY OF LINOTYPE-HELL AG
DIN VARIATIONS DESIGNED BY GRAPHIC LANGUAGE
ALL OTHER TEXT + IMAGES BY GRAPHIC LANGUAGE

WWW.KRABBESHOLM.DK
WWW.PROTOTYPE-EDITIONS.COM

A B C

D E F

DIN 1451 ENGSCHRIFT ©1936 BERTHOLD/LINOTYPE LIBRARY

G H I

J K L